For David and Violet
—W. L.

For the wondrous avian dinosaurs around the world
and the people who protect, study, and enjoy them
—B. Z. G.

With thanks to Laura Godwin, Julia Sooy, and Patrick Collins
for their inspired and creative work on this book
—B. Z. G.

Henry Holt and Company, LLC, *Publishers since 1866*
175 Fifth Avenue, New York, New York 10010 • mackids.com

Henry Holt® is a registered trademark of Henry Holt and Company, LLC.

Library of Congress Cataloging-in-Publication Data
Guiberson, Brenda Z., author.
Feathered dinosaurs / Brenda Z. Guiberson ; illustrated by William Low.—First edition.
pages   cm
Summary: "A beautiful exploration of recently discovered feathered dinosaurs—the ancient ancestors of birds today!"—Provided by publisher.
Audience: Ages 4–8.
ISBN 978-0-8050-9828-0 (hardcover)
1. Dinosaurs—Juvenile literature. 2. Feathers—Juvenile literature. 3. Birds—Origin—Juvenile literature. I. Low, William, illustrator. II. Title.
QE861.5.G846 2016   567.9—dc23   2015003535

Henry Holt books may be purchased for business or promotional use. For information on bulk purchases, please contact the
Macmillan Corporate and Premium Sales Department at (800) 221-7945 x5442 or by e-mail at specialmarkets@macmillan.com.

First Edition—2016 / Designed by Patrick Collins
The paintings for this book were created using oils and acrylic paint on paper.
Printed in China by Toppan Leefung Printing Ltd., Dongguan City, Guangdong Province

1 3 5 7 9 10 8 6 4 2

FEATHERED DINOSAURS

BRENDA Z. GUIBERSON ✦ illustrated by WILLIAM LOW

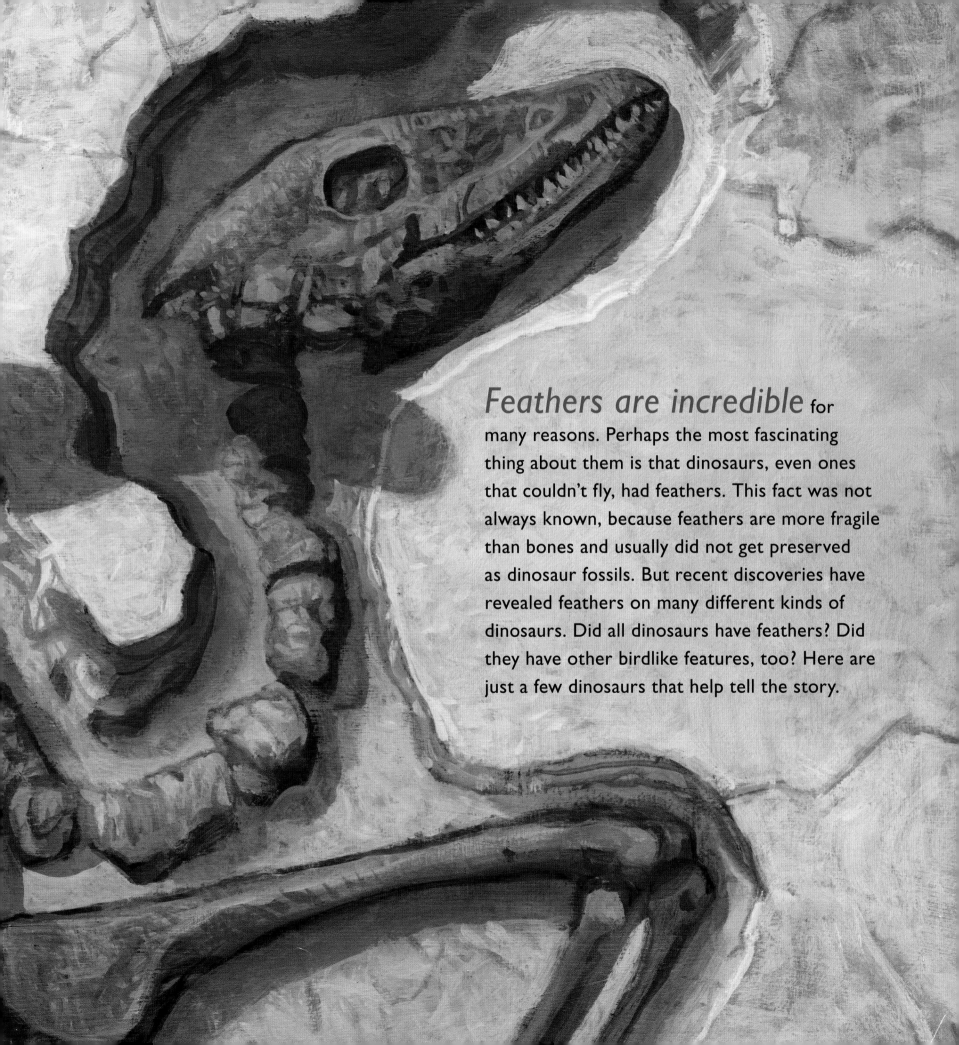

Feathers are incredible for many reasons. Perhaps the most fascinating thing about them is that dinosaurs, even ones that couldn't fly, had feathers. This fact was not always known, because feathers are more fragile than bones and usually did not get preserved as dinosaur fossils. But recent discoveries have revealed feathers on many different kinds of dinosaurs. Did all dinosaurs have feathers? Did they have other birdlike features, too? Here are just a few dinosaurs that help tell the story.

Herrerasaurus (huh-RER-uh-SOR-uhss), which means "Herrera's lizard," was one of the earliest dinosaurs. It is not known if this dinosaur had feathers. During a time when there was less oxygen in the air, Herrerasaurus could breathe better than other creatures, allowing it to run fast on two legs. Its forelimbs were freed up to develop muscles and grasping fingers, giving this carnivore a big advantage over the slow four-legged reptiles and mammals it caught and ate.

Anchiornis (an-kee-OR-niss) means "almost bird." It displayed many of the same traits as modern birds. With fused wrist bones, its arms could fold like a bird folds its wings, hands pointing back and in toward the body. A wishbone—a Y-shaped bone spanning the chest—helped support and strengthen those arms. Though it could not fly, Anchiornis had soft, fluffy feathers and strong flight feathers, too. Scientists have found well-preserved fossils of these feathers with pigment cells called melanosomes that reveal the creature's true beautiful coloring.

Archaeopteryx (ar-kee-AHP-tuh-rikss), which means "ancient wing," has long been considered one of the first birds. Like a modern bird, it had wings with flight feathers, a wishbone, an advanced brain, and clawed feet. Like a dinosaur, it had a toe claw—a larger, curved talon on its second toe, used for slashing and stabbing—as well as a long, bony tail and other bones identical to those of the two-legged dinosaurs called theropods. It also had sharp teeth that were great for catching dragonflies.

Microraptor (MIGH-kroh-rap-tuhr) means "small thief." This little dinosaur had flight feathers on both arms and legs to give it four wings. Some of the feathers were shiny and iridescent. A black coloring on the tips of these feathers came from pigment cells, which added structural strength and helped make it possible for this creature to glide through the air. It had claws designed for climbing, a long tail, and sharp teeth to snatch up insects.

Sinosauropteryx (SIGH-noh-sohr-UHP-teh-rikss), which means "Chinese dragon wing," was a small dinosaur that couldn't fly. It had a beautiful, eye-catching orange-and-white-striped tail. Its colors are known today because archaeologists have discovered preserved feathers containing melanosomes, whose different shapes correspond with different colors. While some dinosaurs of its time were eating the new flowering plants, this dinosaur was a fast, two-legged carnivore. Scientists found the remains of one Sinosauropteryx with its last meal, a mammal, preserved in its belly.

Caudipteryx (kaw-DIP-tuh-rikss) means "tail feather." This dinosaur had a short tail with feathers that were too weak for flying but were quite attractive. Although it had a few teeth in its upper beak, Caudipteryx was a gulper: It swallowed its food whole without chewing. Fossils were found with stones in the gut. Modern toothless birds that can't chew also swallow stones to help them grind food in their gizzards.

Mei long (MAY-lohn), which means "soundly sleeping dragon," was found sleeping like a modern bird. Its head was tucked under a wing with long, clawed fingers. Modern birds, which are warm-blooded, snooze like this to keep warm. Scientists have long believed that dinosaurs were cold-blooded, like reptiles. But does Mei long's sleeping pose mean that some ancient dinosaurs were warm-blooded, too? Researchers are trying to answer this question.

Citipati (CHI-ti-puh-tee) means "funeral pyre lord." This birdlike dinosaur was found sitting on a ground nest over a circle of twenty-two eggs. With legs folded under its body and wings spread wide to protect the eggs, it displayed a brooding behavior similar to that of some modern birds. It also had long hand claws and a toothless beak like a parrot's.

Yutyrannus huali (yoo-ti-RAN-nuhss HWAH-lee) was as long as a school bus, weighed three thousand pounds, and walked on two clawed feet. Before its discovery, few thought such a large dinosaur could have had feathers, but its name means "beautiful feathered tyrant" for a reason. This dinosaur lived in a time of cooler weather and was covered with shaggy six-inch feathers, which helped it keep warm. With a huge body and small arms, this big creature was not a flier.

Tyrannosaurus rex

(tuh-ran-nuh-SOR-uhss REKSS) means "tyrant lizard king." It was a carnivore with tiny arms and very big teeth. But still it had some birdlike features. It had a wishbone and clawed feet. It had blood vessels similar to ostriches' and quickly grew from baby to its full, twelve-thousand-pound adult size. And like modern female birds, it had special calcium-rich bones to make strong eggshells.

Hesperornis (hes-puh-ROHR-nuhss), the "western bird," was a diving dinosaur as large as a man. It had teeny wings to keep it streamlined underwater and huge feet for steering in the cool seaway that once flooded the middle of North America. Its jaws were lined with sharp teeth that could grab fish. It could not fly, and it walked awkwardly, too.

Confuciusornis (kuhn-FYOO-shuh-SOHR-nuhss) means "Confucius bird." This prehistoric bird was the first known to have a toothless beak. It was also the first to have a pygostyle—a fused bone at the end of its spine—instead of a tail. Several hundred complete fossils of this bird were found in China. Only some of them had long tail feathers that were not flight feathers. Their clawed arms were extra long to help them fly.

Eoalulavis (yee-oh-uh-LOO-luh-viss) means "early small winged bird." It was the first known bird to have an alula, a small, thumb-like extension on its wing, as modern birds have. The extra flight feathers on this thumb allowed Eoalulavis to maneuver at slow speeds; they also helped with controlled flight during takeoff and landing. The size of a sparrow, this smart bird was a skilled flier.

With recent discoveries, it now seems that many dinosaurs had at least some feathers. But only a few of these—the avian dinosaurs—survived and evolved to become modern birds. Congratulations to geese, robins, hummingbirds, and almost ten thousand other species that continue the age of dinosaurs in our backyard.

Small and Smart, Fast and Feathered

Dinosaur discoveries are happening with great frequency these days. Surprising preservations that include feathers have been found around ancient lake beds and volcanic ash deposits in China. These fossils revealed feathers on many different kinds of dinosaurs all related to the theropods. In 2014, an expedition in Siberia uncovered an ornithischian dinosaur, part of a group very different from theropods, that had feathers, too. This discovery hints that possibly all dinosaurs had feathers for at least part of their lives.

The dinosaurs used their feathers to keep warm or to attract mates. Some had feathers on both arms and legs and could glide like a biplane. Some dinosaurs exhibited birdlike behavior with nests and eggs. Some of the bird ancestors had tails, teeth, and claws like other dinosaurs did. At times it would be hard to know who was the dinosaur and who was the bird. Eventually, the small, smart, fast dinosaurs with strong flight feathers became the birds. Recent research also suggests that some avian dinosaurs survived the mass extinction because of the shape of their eggs.

Bird ancestors related to the theropods underwent twelve big decreases in size that led to Archaeopteryx and other ancient birds. They were evolving at a rate four times faster than other dinosaurs. They lost teeth and tails, which made them more lightweight for flying. Long, flapping arms helped them leap and climb. Strong flight feathers, big brains, and excellent eyes allowed them to zip through the air and hunt at night. A reversed first toe enabled them to perch on tree limbs.

The ancient birds could fly up or away to avoid predators. When sea levels dropped and continents drifted, they could reach new islands and find extra food. While the slow-adapting huge dinosaurs were becoming extinct, the avian dinosaurs—the birds—were the survivors. Today this beautiful, varied, and successful group can be found on every continent on Earth.

Bibliography

ABRAMSON, ANDRA SERLIN, JASON BROUGHAM, AND CARL MEHLING. *Inside Dinosaurs*. New York: Sterling, 2010.

ARNOLD, CAROLINE. *Dinosaurs with Feathers: The Ancestors of Modern Birds*. New York: Clarion Books, 2001.

BAKKER, ROBERT, PH.D. *The Dinosaur Heresies*. New York: Morrow, 1986.

BALTER, MICHAEL. "Flight School." *Audubon*. (January/February 2015): 22–29.

DINGUS, LOWELL AND TIMOTHY ROWE. *The Mistaken Extinction: Dinosaur Evolution and the Origin of Birds*. New York: W. H. Freeman, 1998.

DIXON, DOUGAL. *Dinosaurs*, 3rd ed. Honesdale, PA: Boyds Mills Press, 2007.

FEDUCCIA, ALAN. *Riddle of the Feathered Dragons: Hidden Birds of China*. New Haven: Yale University Press, 2012.

GARDOM, TIM AND ANGELA MILNER. *The Natural History Museum Book of Dinosaurs*. London: Carlton Books LTD, 2006.

HALLS, KELLY MILNER. *Dinosaur Mummies: Beyond Bare-Bone Fossils*. Plain City, OH: Darby Creek Publishing, 2003.

JOHNSTON, MARIANNE. *From the Dinosaurs of the Past to the Birds of the Present*. New York: Rosen Publishing Group, 2000.

LONG, JOHN AND PETER SCHOUTEN. *Feathered Dinosaurs: The Origin of Birds*. New York: Oxford University Press, 2008.

MANNING, PHILLIP. *Grave Secrets of Dinosaurs: Soft Tissues and Hard Science*. Washington, DC: National Geographic, 2008.

MORELL, VIRGINIA. "The Origin of Birds: Is There a Dinosaur Link?" *Audubon* (March/April 1997): 36–45.

PAUL, GREGORY S. *Dinosaurs of the Air: The Evolution and Loss of Flight in Dinosaurs and Birds*. Baltimore: Johns Hopkins University Press, 2002.

PAUL, GREGORY S. *The Princeton Field Guide to Dinosaurs*. Princeton, NJ: Princeton University Press, 2010.

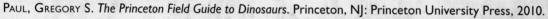

PEARSON, HELEN. "Raising the Dead." *Nature* 483 (March 22, 2012): 390–393.

SAMPSON, SCOTT D. *Dinosaur Odyssey: Fossil Threads in the Web of Life.* Berkeley: University of California Press, 2009.

SCHOMP, VIRGINIA. *Archaeopteryx and Other Flying Dinosaurs.* New York: Marshall Cavendish, 2004.

SHEALY, DENNIS R. *Dinosaurs Alive!: The Dinosaur-Bird Connection.* New York: Random House, 2001.

SLOAN, CHRISTOPHER. *How Dinosaurs Took Flight: Fossils, Science, What We Think We Know, and Mysteries Yet Unsolved.* Washington, DC: National Geographic, 2005.

WARD, PETER D. *Out of Thin Air: Dinosaurs, Birds, and Earth's Ancient Atmosphere.* Washington, DC: Joseph Henry Press, 2006.